197

 St. Louis Community College

Forest Park
Florissant Valley
Meramec

Instructional Resources
St. Louis, Missouri

GAYLORD

VERGIL'S Eclogues

ECLO
Vergil's

GUES

Translated by Barbara Hughes Fowler

The University of North Carolina Press *Chapel Hill & London*

© 1997

The University of
North Carolina Press

All rights reserved

Designed by
Richard Hendel

Set in Minion type
by Eric M. Brooks

Manufactured in the
United States of America

The paper in this book
meets the guidelines for
permanence and durability
of the Committee on
Production Guidelines for
Book Longevity of the
Council on Library
Resources.

Library of Congress Cataloging-in-Publication Data

Virgil.

[Bucolica. English]

Vergil's Eclogues / translated by Barbara Hughes Fowler.

p. cm.

ISBN 0-8078-2347-3 (cloth: alk. paper). —

ISBN 0-8078-4653-8 (pbk.: alk. paper)

1. Pastoral poetry, Latin — Translations into English.

2. Country life — Rome — Poetry.

I. Fowler, Barbara Hughes, 1926– .

II. Title.

PA6807.B7F69   1997

872'.01 — dc21   96-36990

CIP

01 00 99 98 97   5 4 3 2 1

With great affection,

I dedicate this book

to my fellow members of

our own Joy Luck Club:

CHRISTINA CLARK,

POLLY HOOVER,

and

JENNIFER LARSON

Contents

Acknowledgments

I wish to thank Eugene Bushala and Ernst Fredricksmeyer,

who read my manuscript and made many valuable observations;

Polly Hoover, who helped in more ways than she can know to

make this little book possible; and, once more, my wonderful editors,

Barbara Hanrahan and Ron Maner, at the University of North

Carolina Press.

Introduction

Publius Vergilius Maro was born on October 15, 70 B.C., at Andes, a village near Mantua in Cisalpine Gaul (northern Italy), where his father owned a small farm. He was educated at Cremona and Milan and is said to have studied later at Naples with Parthenius of Bithynia, who taught him Greek, and at Rome with the Epicurean philosopher Siro and the rhetorician Epidius. He may after that have returned home and composed the early works that are usually attributed to him: *Ciris, Copa, Culex, Dirae,* and *Moretum.*

Octavian and Mark Antony, who defeated Brutus and Cassius at Philippi in 42 B.C., had promised their veterans lands in Italy. As a result, in 41 B.C. Vergil's father was threatened with the loss of his property. At the urging of C. Asinius Pollio, then governor of Cisalpine Gaul, and his successor, L. Alfenus Varus, the young Vergil appealed to Octavian on his father's behalf. His suit was successful, and *Eclogue I* is a gracious acknowledgment of Octavian's favor.

It was Pollio who, according to Servius, the ancient commentator on Vergil (ca. 400 A.D.), persuaded Vergil to try his hand at pastoral verse. Vergil then composed the *Eclogues* in a period of three years, publishing them at the age of twenty-seven. The *Eclogues,* Servius also tells us, were not composed in the order in which they appear in the published collection, and that much is obvious. *Eclogue IX,* for instance, was written after confiscations of land near Mantua and Cremona and is apparently an appeal to Varus to save Vergil's father's farm (part of the efforts that led Varus to join Pollio in encouraging Vergil to plead his father's cause with Octavian directly). *Eclogue I* was obviously written after the farm had been saved. Beyond that we cannot be certain of even relative dates. Then too the notional date of a poem may not have been the date of composition. Attempts to explain the arrangement of the poems in the collection have been many, but none is conclusive. After the publication of the *Eclogues,* Vergil lived chiefly in Rome, where he enjoyed the patronage of Octavian's minister Maecenas. With Maecenas's encouragement, between 37 and 30 B.C. he composed the *Georgics.*

We know little of Vergil's personal life. He is said to have been tall and dark, and to have been, because of ill health and devotion to his work, a recluse so painfully shy that he would, when recognized, take shelter in the nearest available house. He once pleaded a case at law. We have a glimpse of him in 37 B.C. on the famous "Journey to Brundisium" (Horace, *Satires I.5*), when Horace was suffering from sore eyes and Vergil from indigestion. After ten years of work on the *Aeneid*, Vergil planned a trip to the Near East to visit the sites of his poem, but he was taken ill on the journey at Megara in Greece. He turned back and had barely reached Brundisium in Italy when he died on September 22, 19 B.C. He had hoped to spend three more years on his *Aeneid*, and his dying request was that the unfinished poem be burned. Instead the Emperor Augustus gave it to his friends Varius Rufus and Plotius Tucca to edit, and it was published in about 17 B.C.

The *Eclogues* ("selections"), or, as Vergil called them, *Bucolica*, are pastorals, a form of poetry first known to us in the work of the Greek poet Theocritus (fl. ca. 280 B.C.), who was probably born on the Aegean island of Cos, spent his early life in Sicily, and worked in Alexandria. His *Idylls* ("small sketches") are charming and amusing pictures of life in an idealized countryside where shepherds and goatherds engage in singing contests. Their songs are usually about love, of boys for girls, or of boys for boys. It was these that Vergil set out to imitate, and indeed there are echoes of Theocritus's work throughout the *Eclogues*, whether in the general structure and subject matter of a particular poem or in the paraphrasing or actual translation of individual lines.

Despite the obvious borrowings from Theocritus, Vergil's *Eclogues* are not at all Theocritean. Theocritus's *Idylls*, though sometimes set in Sicily or Cos, generally reflect the flora of the eastern Mediterranean, where he must have traveled. Vergil's *Eclogues* are for the most part set in an imaginary Arcadia which is also at times his native Italian countryside. In *Eclogue VII*, for instance, the Mincio, a river of Cisalpine Gaul, appears, nonsensically—and nobody cares—in Arcadia. The *Eclogues* abound in Greek place names, but there is mention too of Mantua and Cremona, towns near Vergil's native Andes. There are also, as there are not in Theocritus's pastorals, references to contemporary political figures and events: Pollio, Varus, Octavian; the deification of Julius Caesar; the confiscations by the triumvirs of the lands around Mantua and Cremona. Vergil takes the names of most of his fictional characters from Theocritus, but those characters are not, with one exception (Galataea in *Eclogue IX*) the same people that they were in the *Idylls*.

Theocritus's shepherds, cowherds, and goatherds speak in a highly artificial Doric dialect. Vergil's shepherds speak, with the exception of a few colloquial words, a standard literary Latin. In the end, no matter what Vergil borrowed from his Greek predecessor, no matter how many Greek settings and names he used, his poems are unmistakably Italian and in some respects Roman.

The greatest difference between Theocritus's *Idylls* and Vergil's *Eclogues* is, however, in the versification. Both poets wrote in dactylic hexameter, a six-foot line composed of dactyls (¯ ˘ ˘) and spondees (¯ ¯). Both Latin and Greek verse are quantitative. Scansion depends not upon accent, as it does in English verse, but upon quantity, that is, the actual length of time it takes to pronounce a syllable. In English verse quantity does play a secondary role. We are slowed in our pronunciation by long vowels and consonant clusters, and we do sometimes consciously so compose. So also in Latin the natural stress of the words played a counterpart to the quantity of the syllables: they might or they might not coincide. Greek was, however, a tone language, in which pitch played in counterpart to quantity. Greek has an immense array of particles and pronouns, little words that could make a long but delicate line. Latin has no articles and no real particles. The Greek verbal system is extensive and highly flexible. Latin has far more constricted paradigms and a relatively inflexible syntax. Greek has an almost limitless vocabulary; the Latin vocabulary is comparatively restricted. Greek is strong in vowels; Latin, like English, in consonants. The miracle of Latin verse is the sophistication, subtlety, and wonderful sonorousness that Roman poets could, with their intractable language, achieve.

I have translated these poems in a basically iambic six-foot line, allowing myself the conventional substitutions: anapests, trochees, tribrachs, and the occasional syncopated foot. In a few instances involving proper names I have allowed a hypermetric syllable. All but the most obvious proper nouns (e.g., Rome) are explained in my notes. I have for the most part followed the text of W. Clausen, *A Commentary on Vergil, Eclogues* (Oxford, 1994). I am also indebted to Clausen for many of my notes.

VERGIL'S Eclogues

ECLOGUE I

Meliboeus, Tityrus

M. Tityrus, you lie beneath the spreading beech
    and practice country songs upon a slender pipe.
    I leave my father's fields and my sweet ploughlands,
    an exile from my native soil. You sprawl in the shade
    and school the woods to sound with Amaryllis's charms.   5
T. O Meliboeus, it was a god who gave me this repose.
    He'll always be a god to me. Often I'll stain
    his altar with blood of a young lamb from my fold. He
    it was who allowed my cattle to graze like this and me
    to play the songs I choose upon my rustic flute.   10
M. I'm not jealous of you. I'm merely surprised. All
    around the farms are so disturbed. I'm tired and yet
    I drive my goats on. This one I scarcely drag,
    for in the hazel thicket there she's just dropped twins,
    the hope of the flock, and abandoned them on the bare flint. 15
    Had my wits not been so slow, I'd surely have known
    that the lightning-struck oaks predicted this for us.
    But still, tell me, Tityrus, who is this god of yours?
T. Meliboeus, I thought that that city they call Rome—
    I was such a fool—was just like that town of ours   20
    where often we shepherds drive the tender lambs from our flock.
    Puppies were like dogs and kids like nanny goats,
    I knew, and so I would compare big things to small.
    But this city stands as far above the rest
    as the cypress outgrows the trailing hedgerow.   25
M. Why were you so eager to go visiting Rome?
T. Liberty. I'd been lazy. It called me late—
    not until the clippings fell whiter from my beard.
    Still it came. After all that time the call came,
    after Amaryllis had captured me, and Galataea   30

had abandoned me. For I confess that while
I was so mad for Galataea I had no hope
of liberty, nor did I save my wages for that.
Though many a sacrificial lamb went out from my pens
and many a rich cheese from my press to the thankless town,   35
I never came home with money heavy in my hand.

M. I wondered, Amaryllis, why your prayers were so sad,
and for whose sake you let your apples hang on the tree.
Tityrus had gone. Tityrus, the pines
themselves, the very springs, the vineyards were calling for you.   40

T. What could I do? I couldn't free myself or find
such protective gods anywhere else but there.
There I saw that young man, Meliboeus, for whom
my altars will smoke twice six days of every year.
He it was who gave a prompt reply to my suit: 45
"Graze your cattle again and put your bulls to stud."

M. Fortunate old man, your fields will still be yours.
And they're enough for you although the bare rock
and the marsh with all its reeds and mud abut your fields.
No unfamiliar fodder will tempt your pregnant ewes,   50
nor will any disease from a neighbor's flock bring harm to them.
Fortunate old man, here between the rivers
you know and the sacred springs you'll lie in the cool shade.
Here your hedge, as it always has, at your neighbor's line
will pasture on willow buds those Hyblaean bees,   55
which soon will coax you to sleep with their light murmuring hum.
There beneath the high rock the vinedresser
will sing to the breeze and all the while your hoarse pigeons
and your turtle dove, high in the elm, will murmur and coo.

T. And so, the swift stags will pasture in upper air   60
and the straits of the sea abandon fish, bare on the shore,
and wandering both beyond the boundaries of each,
the banished Parthian will drink from the river Arar
and Germany from the Babylonian Tigris's stream
before the memory of his countenance slips from my heart.   65

M. But the rest of us must go to thirsty Africa
or Scythia and the rapid Oaxes's chalky stream,
or else to Britain, cut off from us by the width of the world.
Oh, will I ever in any time to come, look
with wonder at a land I can at last call   70
my own, see my modest cottage, its roof heaped
with turf, and after a while, behold my kingdom, my rows
of grain? Is some rough soldier to have these furrowed fields?
Some foreigner these crops? What misery civil strife
has brought to us Romans! For such as these have we sown
   this land!   75
Now graft your pears, Meliboeus, now plant your vines in rows.
Get on my goats, once a happy flock, get on.
Never again as I lie in some green cave
will I see you dangling from a distant brambled cliff.
I shall sing no songs, nor shall I pasture you, my goats,   80
on the flowering clover and on the bitter willow shoots.
T. But still, you could stop here with me this one night,
sleep on a bed of green leaves. I have ripe apples,
soft chestnuts, and a fine supply of pressed cheese.
And now, over there, the roofs of the farms begin to smoke,   85
and the shadows fall farther from the tops of the high hills.

ECLOGUE II

The shepherd Corydon was burning for lovely Alexis,
who was his master's love. There was no hope for him.
And so he'd go to where the thick beeches spread
their canopy of shade, and all alone he'd sing,
helplessly, to wood and hills these shreds of song: 5
"O cruel Alexis, don't you care at all for my tunes?
Nor pity me in the least? In the end will you drive me to death?
Now even cattle seek the cool relief of the shade,
and even the green lizards hide in the thornbrake,
and Thestylis, for the reapers, wearied by the fierce heat,   10
is pounding garlic and wild thyme for a fragrant brew.
But together with me, while I trace out your steps,
beneath the scorching sun, the harsh cicada makes
the orchards ring. Wasn't it better to put up
with Amaryllis's sulky moods and haughty airs,   15
or Menalcas, dark though he is and you so fair? Don't trust
O, beautiful boy, too much in lovely hue. The pale
privet falls. The dusky hyacinth is plucked.
Alexis, you despise me, nor do you ask me who
I am, how many flocks I have, how rich I am   20
in snowy milk. A thousand lambs of mine range
Sicilian hills. I've a fine supply of fresh milk
all the summer long and in the winter too.
I can sing as Amphion of Dirce used to sing
on Actaean Aracynthus when he'd call the cattle home.   25
And I'm not so ugly. Lately I saw myself at the shore
when the sea stood still of the wind. You could compare me
with Daphnis—I'd have no fear—if mirrors never lie.
If only you'd live with me in the rough countryside
in a low-lying hut and shoot stags with me and herd   30
my flock of goats with a green marsh-mallow switch.
If you sing with me in the woods, you'll learn to rival Pan.

Pan taught us first to join a set of reeds with wax.
Pan cares for sheep and for the men who tend the sheep.
Don't be annoyed if you rub your delicate lip on the reed.   35
What didn't Amyntas do to learn this very art?
I have a pipe of seven graded hemlock stalks.
Damoetas, long ago, as he lay dying, said,
when he gave it to me, 'You, now, are its second lord.'
So Damoetas said, and Amyntas was jealous, fool   40
that he was. Besides, I found in a dangerous ravine
two chamois goats, their pelts dappled yet with white.
Twice a day they suck their ewe dry. For you
I'm saving them, though Thestylis keeps begging me
for them. And she'll succeed in getting them, since   45
my gifts seem paltry to you. O lovely boy, come, see:
the nymphs bring baskets of lilies for you. The glowing naiad,
plucking pale violets for you and poppy-heads,
binds narcissus to fragrant bud of anise plant,
then plaits the cassia with other sweet-smelling herbs, and tints   50
the tender hyacinth with tawny marigold.
I myself shall gather quinces with downy bloom,
and chestnuts, which my Amaryllis used to love.
I'll add waxen plums. This fruit shall be honored too.
And you, O laurels, I'll pluck, and the neighboring myrtle too,   55
for, planted side by side, your lovely perfumes blend.
Corydon, you're a boor. Alexis scorns your gifts.
Nor will Iollas, if you contend with him
in gifts, concede. What misery have I brought on myself?
I've allowed the South Wind to wither my flowering plants,   60
and I've allowed the wild boars at my clear springs.
Fool, from whom do you run? Gods too have lived
in the woods, and Paris of Troy. Let Pallas Athene dwell
inside the citadels she builds. Let us enjoy
the woods. The savage lioness pursues the wolf;   65
the wolf, the kid; the gambolling kid, the flowering clover;
and Corydon, you, Alexis. Desire draws each one on.
Look, the oxen carry their plows aslant from the yoke,

and the setting sun doubles all the shadows' length.
But love burns me still. What help is there for love? 70
Corydon, Corydon, what is this madness that's taken you?
Your vine is half-pruned on the thick-leaved elm.
Why don't you do instead a useful piece of work?
Plait a basket with pliant reeds and osier twigs?
If he despises you, you'll find another Alexis." 75

ECLOGUE III

Menalcas, Damoetas, Palaemon

M. Tell me, Damoetas, whose flock is this? Meliboeus's?

D. Aegon's rather. He recently handed it over to me.

M. O sheep, forever unfortunate flock! While the master
    cuddles Neaera and worries lest she prefer me
    to him, a stranger's hand milks them twice an hour.   5
    The flock is robbed of sustenance, the lambs of their milk.

D. Take care, nevertheless, that you jibe more sparingly
    at men. We know with whom while the billy goats watched
    and in what little shrine—but the tolerant nymphs merely laughed.

M. Then, I think, when they saw me slashing Micon's orchard   10
    and tender nursery shoots with my wicked pruning hook.

D. Or here near the ancient beeches when you broke Daphnis's
    bow and reeds. When you saw that the boy had got them, you grieved,
    and had died, willful Menalcas, had you not done him harm.

M. What are masters to do when thieves dare such?   15
    Did I not see you, scoundrel, snatching Damon's goat
    from ambush while Lycisca barked loud and long?
    And when I shouted, "Where's that rogue off to now?
    Tityrus, herd the flock!" you hid behind the sedge.

D. But when I'd won in singing, that rascal wouldn't give me   20
    the goat that I'd won with my pipe and songs. And in case
    you don't know, that goat was mine. Damon himself
    admitted it but said that he couldn't give it up.

M. You conquered him in singing? Or did you have a pipe
    compacted with wax? Didn't you usually, dunce,   25
    at the crossroads murder a wretched tune with strident straw?

D. Would you like us to try what each of us in turn can do?
    I pledge this heifer and, lest you hesitate, she comes
    twice to the milking pail and nurses two calves besides
    from her teat. Now tell me what you'll pledge in our contest
        of song.   30

M. I dare not pledge a single thing from the flock to you,
    for I have a wicked stepmother and a father at home.
    Both count the flock twice a day, and one the kids,
    but that which you'll confess is better by far I'll pledge
    (since you insist upon insanity), cups   35
    of beechwood, the engraved work of divine Alcimedon,
    on which a pliant vine laid on by skillful lathe
    cloaks the clusters the pale ivy spreads about.
    In the middle two figures, Conon, and who was the other
    who marked with his rod the entire orb of heaven for men,   40
    what seasons the reaper and which the bent ploughman should keep?
    Not yet have I put my lip to them. I keep them hid.

D. Alcimedon made two cups for me as well
    and wreathed the handles round with tender acanthus stems.
    Orpheus he put in the center and the following woods.   45
    Not yet have I put my lip to them. I keep them hid.
    If you look at the calf, you can't possibly praise the cups.

M. You'll not escape from me today. I'll go wherever you call—
    only let someone hear—he who comes, Palaemon.
    I'll see that after this your voice will challenge none.   50

D. But come, if you have anything. There'll be no delay
    in me. I shrink from no one. Only, neighbor Palaemon,
    take this well to heart. The matter is nothing small.

P. Sing on, now that we are seated in the soft grass
    and all the field and every tree is burgeoning.   55
    Now the woods are in leaf, the year at its loveliest.
    Damoetas, begin. Then, Menalcas, you follow after him.
    You'll sing in alternation—that's what the Muses love.

D. From Jove is the Muses' beginning. All is full of Jove.
    He cultivates the lands. He cherishes my songs.   60

M. And Phoebus loves me. Gifts for Phoebus I always have,
    the laurel trees and the sweetly blushing hyacinth.

D. Galataea pelts me with an apple, the saucy girl,
    then rushes to the willows wanting first to be seen.

M. My flame, Amyntas, comes to me of his own accord   65
    so that Delia now is not better known to our dogs.

D. I've got gifts for my lover, for I have marked the spot
      where the wood pigeons have built their nests high above.

M. What I could I sent to the boy, plucked from the tree—
      ten golden apples. Tomorrow I'll send ten more.   70

D. How often and sweetly has Galataea spoken to me.
      O winds, carry some part of her words to the ears of the gods!

M. What use if you don't scorn me in your heart, Amyntas,
      if, while you pursue the boar, I tend the nets?

D. Send my Phyllis to me. It is my birthday, Iollas.   75
      When I offer a calf for the crops, come yourself.

M. I love Phyllis before the others. She wept when I left
      and said, "A long goodbye, my comely one, Iollas."

D. Disastrous the wolf to the pens, rains to the ripe grain,
      winds to the trees, and Amaryllis's anger to me.   80

M. Moisture is sweet to the crops, arbutus to weanling kids,
      the pliant willow to pregnant herd, Amyntas to me.

D. Pollio loves our Muse, rustic though she is.
      Pierides, pasture a calf for your reader Pollio.

M. But Pollio composes new songs. Pasture a bull   85
      soon to strike with his horn and scatter sand with his feet.

D. Let your lover, Pollio, come where you rejoice.
      Let honey flow for him and the rough bramble bear balsam.

M. Who doesn't hate Bavius, let him love your songs, Maevius,
      and let him yoke foxes and milk the billy goats.   90

D. O lads who gather flowers and strawberries from the ground,
      flee from here. A cold snake hides in the grass.

M. Careful, my sheep, don't go too far. You can't trust
      the bank. The ram himself is now drying his fleece.

D. Tityrus, drive the pasturing sheep from the river bank.   95
      I'll wash them all myself in the spring when the time comes.

M. Herd the sheep, my lads. If the heat steals the milk
      as recently it did, we'll press their udders in vain.

D. Alas, alas, how lean is my bull in the rich vetch!
      The same love is death to the cowherd and the herd.   100

M. These certainly—nor is love to blame—scarcely cling
      to their bones. Some evil eye bewitches my tender lambs.

D.   Say in what lands—you'll be mighty Apollo
     to me—the space of the sky is three cubits, no more.
M.   Say in what lands the names of kings are inscribed   105
     on blossoming buds and keep Phyllis for yourself.
P.   It's beyond me to resolve the contest between you.
     You both deserve the calf, and anyone else who
     shall fear a sweet love or taste its bitter fruit.
     Shut off the streams, my lads. The meadows have drunk enough.   110

ECLOGUE IV

Sicilian Muses, let us sing a nobler theme.
Orchards and humble tamarisk do not please all.
If we sing of woods, let them be woods fit for a consul.
    The last age of the Cumaean Sybil's song has come.
The mighty sequence of ages is born and begins anew.   5
Now the Maiden returns. The reign of Saturn returns.
Now a new generation descends from heaven on high.
At the birth of the child in whose time the iron race
shall cease and a golden race inherit the whole earth,
smile, O chaste Lucina: now your Apollo reigns.   10
In your consulate this glorious age begins,
Pollio, and the mighty months begin their solemn march.
With you whatever traces of our guilt remain
will vanish and loose the world from its perpetual fear.
He will consort with the gods and see heroes mingling   15
with them and he himself will appear to heroes and gods
and rule a world his father's virtues have brought to peace.
    For you, little child, spontaneously, as first gifts,
the earth will lavish creeping ivy and foxglove,
everywhere, and Egyptian lilies with smiling acanthus.   20
Goats will come home by themselves with udders full
of milk, nor will the oxen fear the lion's might.
Your very cradle will flower with buds to caress you.
The serpent will die as well as poison's treacherous plant,
and everywhere Assyrian balsam will come to bloom.   25
And when you have learned to read the praises of heroes and deeds
of your own father and know what manhood is, the plain,
little by little, will grow gold with waving grain,
and grapes will redden on the untended vine of the thorn,
and the hard oaks distill honey-dew from their barks.   30
Still, slight traces of our old iniquity
will make us tempt the sea in ships, fortify

our towns with walls, cut furrows in our soil.
There will be another Tiphys, another Argo's
chosen crew, and there will be other wars, 35
and mighty Achilles will be dispatched once more to Troy.
Later still, when strengthening time has made you a man,
the trader will willingly cease from the sea and the pine ship
to exchange its wares. Each land will produce all its needs.
The soil will not suffer the hoe nor the vine the pruning knife. 40
Then too the sturdy ploughman will loose his bulls from the yoke.
Nor will wool learn to deceive with this hue and that,
but in the meadows the ram himself will change his fleece,
now to a soft sea-purple, now to the yellow of saffron.
Crimson coats will naturally clothe the pasturing lambs. 45
    "Such let the ages run," said the harmonious Fates
to their spindles, with Destiny's unalterable decree.
Now enter upon your glorious career, for the time is at hand,
sweet child of the gods, great increment of Jove.
Look at the world nodding beneath the weight of its dome, 50
at the lands, the tracts of the sea, and the fathomless depths of the sky.
See how all creation takes joy in the age to come!
Oh, if only my final days could be prolonged
and I had left breath enough to tell your deeds,
Thracian Orpheus could not conquer me in song, 55
nor Linus, though he had his mother, he his father with him,
Orpheus, Calliope, Linus, the beautiful Apollo.
If Pan himself, with Arcadia judge, should vie with me,
then Pan himself, with Arcadia judge, would own defeat.
Begin, then, little boy, to know your mother 60
with a smile. Ten long months have left your mother tired.
Begin, little boy: he who has not smiled at his mother
is not worthy of a god's table or a goddess's bed.

ECLOGUE V

Menalcas, Mopsus

ME. Why do we not, Mopsus, since both of us are skilled,
    you at playing slender reeds, I at verse,
    sit down here among the mingled hazels and elms?
MO. You're the elder. It's right that I do what you say, Menalcas,
    whether beneath the flickering shadows that western breezes   5
    chase or in this grotto we take our rest. Look
    how the forest vine sprinkles the cave with sparing clusters.
ME. Upon our hills Amyntas alone contends with you.
MO. What if he strives to surpass Phoebus himself in song?
ME. Begin, Mopsus, be first, if any flame you have   10
    for Phyllis or compliments for Alcon or quarrels with Codrus.
    Begin. Tityrus will care for your pasturing goats.
MO. Rather these songs which recently I wrote upon
    the green bark of beech, marking the times of pipe
    and song. Then you order Amyntas next to compete.   15
ME. As the pliant willow yields to the silvery olive tree,
    as much as low-lying nard to gardens of crimson rose,
    just so much, we judge, does Amyntas yield to you.
    But now no further remarks my lad. We've reached the cave.
MO. For Daphnis, dead by a cruel fate, the nymphs did weep   20
    (witness were you to the nymphs, O rivers and hazel trees),
    when clasping in her arms her son's pathetic corpse,
    his mother called upon the gods and the cruel stars.
    Daphnis, none in those days drove the pastured cows
    to the cool streams. No four-footed beast lapped at the brook   25
    or cropped the meadow grass. Daphnis, the wild hills
    and forests tell how even Punic lions mourned
    at your death. Daphnis was first to order Armenian tigers
    yoked to chariots. Daphnis was also first
    to lead in choruses of Bacchic revelers,   30

their vibrant wands twined with tender foliage.
As the vine embellishes the trees, the grapes the vines,
the bulls the herd, the sown crops the rich fields,
so you your own. After the Fates bore you off,
Pales and Apollo themselves abandoned the fields. 35
In the furrows where often we sowed large barley plants
the barren darnel and fruitless wild oats spring up.
In place of the tender violet or glowing narcissus
there rises the thistle and prickly thorn with its sharp spikes.
Strew the earth with leaves, cover the fountains with shade, 40
shepherds. (Daphnis demands that such be done for him.)
Make a grave mound and on the mound add a song:
"Daphnis I was among the woods, famed to the stars,
guard of a handsome flock and handsomer myself."

ME. Such is your song to us, divine poet, as 45
sleep to the weary upon the grass, as in the heat
the quenching of thirst by the sweet drink from a leaping stream.
With voice as well as reeds you are your master's equal.
Fortunate lad! You will now be second to him.
Nevertheless, we'll sing somehow these songs of ours 50
in turn, exalting your Daphnis to the stars. To the stars
your Daphnis we'll exalt, for Daphnis loved us as well.

MO. What could ever be greater than such a gift to us?
The lad himself was worthy of song, and those songs
of yours Stimichon long ago praised to us. 55

ME. Radiant, Daphnis marvels at the threshold,
unfamiliar beneath his feet, of Olympus, and sees
the clouds and stars, and so lively pleasure fills
the woods and all the countryside and captures too
Pan and shepherds and the dryad maiden nymphs. 60
Neither does the wolf plot ambush for the flock nor
nets treachery for the deer. Kindly Daphnis
loves repose. The forested mountaintops themselves
cast their voices in joy to the stars. The very rocks,
the woods themselves resound with songs. "A god, a god 65
is he, Menalcas!" Be generous to your own. See,

four altars, two for you, Daphnis, and two
for Phoebus. Two cups foaming with new milk each year
and two bowls of olive oil I'll offer to you,
making above all the banquets convivial   70
with much wine, before the hearth if the weather be cold,
if at the harvest time, then in the shade. I'll pour
from goblets a new nectar, fine Ariusian wine.
Damoetas and Lyctian Aegon shall sing their songs to me.
Alphesiboeus shall imitate the leaping satyrs.   75
These rites shall always be yours, both when we properly make
our solemn vows to the nymphs and when we purify
our fields. While the wild boar inhabits the mountain ridge,
the fish the streams, while bees pasture on thyme, while
cicadas on dew, your honor, your name, your praise shall remain.   80
As to Bacchus and Ceres, so to you farmers
shall make their annual vows, and you as well will grant
their prayers and so in turn compel them to keep their vows.

MO. What gift can I return to you for such a song?
For neither the whisper of the coming South Wind   85
nor the shore struck by the wave delights me so, nor streams
that tumble down along the rocky mountain vales.

ME. First I'll give to you this brittle hemlock pipe.
This pipe taught me "Corydon burns for lovely Alexis."
This same pipe "Whose flock is this? Meliboeus's?"   90

MO. But you take this shepherd's crook, which although
he often asked for it (and he was worthy then
of my love) Antigenes did not bear off with him.
It's beautiful, Menalcas, with spaced knots and brass.

ECLOGUE VI

First she deigned to play with Syracusan verse,
nor did my Thalia blush to inhabit the woodlands.
When I was singing of battles and kings, Cynthius
plucked my ear and admonished me. "Tityrus,
a shepherd should pasture fat sheep but a slender song."   5
Now will I (for there will be those, Varus, who long
to sing your praises and celebrate your grim wars)
practice songs of a country Muse with delicate reed.
Not unbidden verses do I sing. If anyone
at all, for love, reads these, our tamarisks will sing   10
of you, Varus, and all the forest too. No page
is dearer to Phoebus than a dedication to Varus.
    Begin, Pierides. The boys, Mnasyllus
and Chromis, saw Silenus lying asleep in a cave,
his veins, as ever before, swollen with yesterday's wine.   15
His garlands, slipped from his head, lay a little way off,
and his heavy jug by its worn handle hung from his hand.
Creeping up (for often the old man had teased
them both with hope of a song), they cast upon him
fetters fashioned from his garlands. Fairest of nymphs,   20
Aegle joins them and overcomes their timidity.
Now his eyes are open, she paints his temples and brow
with mulberries, blood red. Laughing at their trick,
he says, "Why do you tie these bonds? Release me,
boys. It's enough that you seemed able to fetter. Tell   25
the songs that you want. For you there shall be songs. For her
I have in mind another reward." At once he begins.
Then truly you could have seen wild creatures dance,
and fawns in measure, the massive oaks moving their tops.
Not so much does the Parnassian rock rejoice   30
in Phoebus, nor Rhodope and Ismarus in Orpheus.

For he sang how throughout the immense void had been gathered
the seeds of the lands, the air, and the sea, and together with these
those of liquid fire and how from these beginnings
all origins and the young orb of earth coalesced.   35
Then earth began to compact its floor and separate Nereus
as sea and little by little take on the shapes of things.
Now the lands stand amazed at the growing light
of the rising sun. The rains fall as the clouds lift
when forests first begin to burgeon and living beasts   40
wander here and there over the surprised hills.
Next he tells of the stones Pyrrha tossed, the reign
of Saturn, Caucasian vultures and Prometheus's theft. To these
he adds how sailors called for Hylas left at the font
till all the shores echoed with calls of "Hylas, Hylas";   45
and consoles Pasiphaë with love for the snowy bull.
Fortunate had been that girl had herds never
existed! Unhappy maid, what a madness seized you!
Proteus's daughters filled the fields with false lowings,
but none pursued a union so shameful as with beasts   50
even though she had feared the plow upon her neck
and often had sought the horns upon her smooth brow.
But, unhappy maid, now you wander the hills.
He rests his snowy side upon soft hyacinth
and beneath the black ilex munches the pale grass   55
or follows a cow in the large herd. "Close, O nymphs,
Dictaean nymphs, close now the forest glades
so that perhaps my eyes may see the wandering prints
of the bull. Perhaps some cows will lead him home, enticed
by the green grass or following herds to Gortynian yards."   60
Then he sings of the maid who marveled at the apples
of the Hesperides. Then he sings the sisters
of Phaethon bound with the moss of bitter bark
and raises alders from the ground, slender and tall.
Then he sings of how one of the sisters led Gallus who wandered   65
near the streams of Permessus to the Aonian hills

and how all of Phoebus's choir rose to greet the man,
how Linus, the shepherd, in heavenly song, his hair entwined
with flowers and bitter parsley, spoke these words to him:
"The Muses give these reeds to you, accept them now,   70
which once they gave to the Ascraean elder. On them he used
to charm from the mountains sturdy ash trees with his song.
With these let there be told the birth of Grynaean grove
that there be none in which Apollo takes more pride."
Why should I speak of Nisus's Scylla whose story is   75
that with glowing loins girt with barking dogs
she shattered ships of Dulichium in her whirlpool's depths,
ah, and tore their frightened crews with her sea-hounds
or of Tereus's limbs transformed, the banquet which
Philomela prepared for him or by what flight she sought   80
abandoned realms or on what wings the wretched one
hovered before above her own rooftops?
All that happy Eurotas heard before when Phoebus
practiced it and bade the laurels learn by heart
he sings (the valleys, struck, echo to the stars)   85
until there ordered them to gather the sheep in their folds
the evening star appearing above reluctant Olympus.

ECLOGUE VII

Meliboeus, Corydon, Thyrsis

M. Beneath the whispering ilex Daphnis had happened to sit,
and Corydon and Thyrsis had gathered their flocks as one,
Thyrsis his sheep and Corydon his goats, their teats
swollen with milk, both in the blossom of youth, both
Arcadian, prepared to sing and answer in turn.   5
Here, while I protected my delicate myrtles from frost,
my he-goat, lord of the flock, had wandered down, and I spied
Daphnis. When he saw me opposite, he said,
"Quickly come here, O Meliboeus. Your goat is safe
and your kids; and if you have the time, then rest in the shade.   10
Here your oxen will come alone through the meadows to drink.
Here Mincius borders his verdant banks with tender rush
and swarming from the holy oak the bees resound."
What was I to do? I had no Alcippe nor
a Phyllis to shut up at home the weanling lambs,   15
and the contest of Corydon with Thyrsis was no small thing.
Nevertheless I put off my tasks to see their fun.
They began therefore to vie in alternate verse,
for so did the Muses will that they recall their songs.
Corydon these, Thyrsis those in turn composed.   20

C. Libethran Muses, our delight, either grant
me songs like Codrus's (his verses rank next
to those of Phoebus) or, if we cannot all do so,
here this piercing pipe will hang from the sacred pine.

T. Arcadian shepherds, adorn with ivy your blossoming poet   25
that Codrus burst his sides with jealousy, or, if
he praise beyond my pleasure, bind my brow with foxglove
lest a wicked tongue harm the bard to be.

C. This head of a bristling boar little Micon, Delia,
offers you and the branching antlers of a long-lived stag.   30

If this your favor abide, all in smooth marble
you'll stand with crimson buskins bound about your calves.
T.   These cakes and a bowl of milk, Priapus, once a year
are enough to expect, for it's a poor garden you keep.
We've made you of marble now for the present time, but   35
if breeding time fill up the flock, then be of gold.
C.   Nereid Galataea, sweeter to me than thyme
of Hybla, more glowing than the swan, prettier
than pale ivy, when first the pastured bulls return
to the stalls, if you love Corydon at all, then come.   40
T.   May I seem more bitter than Sardinian grass,
more bristly than broom, cheaper than cast up seaweed
if this day has not been longer for me than a year.
If you've any shame, my pastured cattle, go home.
C.   Fountains covered with moss and grass softer than sleep   45
and verdant arbutus that covers you with sparse shade
protect the flock from the solstice. Parching summer comes,
and now the buds swell on the pliant shoots of the vine.
T.   Here is the hearth and resinous pine. Here the fire
is always high and door posts are black with stubborn soot.   50
Here we care as much for Boreas's cold as the wolf
the numbers of the flock or flooding rivers their banks.
C.   Junipers and shaggy chestnuts stand tall
and everywhere apples lie beneath their trees.
Now everything smiles, but if the lovely Alexis were   55
absent from these hills, you'd see the rivers dry.
T.   The field is parched. The grass dies from the tainted air.
Liber begrudges the hills the vine tendrils' shade.
When my Phyllis comes, all the wood will green
and Jupiter descend in heavy happy rains.   60
C.   Alcides loves the poplar most, Iacchus the vine,
lovely Venus the myrtle, and Phoebus his laurel tree.
Phyllis loves the hazel trees. While she loves them,
myrtle will not surpass the hazel nor Phoebus's bay.
T.   The ash is fairest in the forest, in gardens the pine,   65
the poplar beside the streams, on mountain heights the fir.

But, comely Lycidas, if you'd return to me,
the forest ash, the garden pine would yield to you.

M. I remember these songs and vanquished Thyrsis contending in vain.
Since then it's been Corydon, Corydon with me.   70

ECLOGUE VIII

Damon, Alphesiboeus

The Muse of two shepherds, Damon and Alphesiboeus,
at whose contesting the wondering heifer forgot the grass,
at whose song the lynxes stood in astonishment,
and the rivers, altering their currents, stood still,
this Muse of Damon and Alphesiboeus we will sing.   5
   Whether you sail on past the rocks of mighty Timavus
or whether you skim the shore of Illyrian waters, will
ever the day be mine when I can tell of your deeds?
Or will I be able throughout the world to bruit about
your songs which alone deserve the buskin of Sophocles?   10
From you I began. In you I will desist: accept
the songs begun at your command, and about your brow
allow this ivy to twine among the victor's laurel.
   Night's chill shade had scarcely left the sky, when dew
on delicate grass most pleases the flock. Leaning upon   15
his polished olivewood staff, Damon thus began.

D. Lucifer, arise and bring propitious day
    while I, beguiled by unrequited love for Nysa,
    my betrothed, complain, and though I have no profit from
    their witness, I, as I die, call upon the gods.   20
       Begin with me, my flute, the verses of Maenalus.
    Maenalus ever keeps as his own the whispering grove
    and the speaking pines, ever he hears the shepherds' loves
    and Pan who first forbade the idleness of pipes.
       Begin with me, my flute, the verses of Maenalus.   25
    Mopsus wins Nysa. What can lovers not expect?
    Now will gryphons mate with horses. In after time
    the trembling fallow deer will come with hounds to drink.
       Begin with me, my flute, the verses of Maenalus.
    Cut new torches, Mopsus: a bride is brought to you.   30

Bridegroom, scatter the nuts: Vesper abandons Oeta.
    Begin with me, my flute, the verses of Maenalus.
Wedded to a worthy man, while you despise
everyone, and my pipe and my goats are hateful to you,
and my bristly eyebrows and untrimmed beard repel you,   35
and you don't believe that god cares for mortal things—
    Begin with me, my flute, the verses of Maenalus.
In our orchards I saw you, a little girl, gathering
with your mother dewy apples (I was your guide).
I then had become twelve years old, and I could just   40
touch the apples' laden branches from the ground:
I saw, I died, and a wicked madness swept me away.
    Begin with me, my flute, the verses of Maenalus.
Now I know what Love is. The harsh rocks
of Tmaros or Rhodope or the uttermost Garamants   45
gave him birth; no boy is he of our race or of our blood.
    Begin with me, my flute, the verses of Maenalus.
Savage Love taught the mother to spatter her hands
with children's blood. Cruel were you, mother, as well.
Was the mother more cruel or was it that wicked boy?   50
It was that wicked boy. The mother was cruel too.
    Begin with me, my flute, the verses of Maenalus.
Now let the wolf flee the sheep, sturdy oaks
bear apples of gold; with narcissus let the alder bloom,
and let the rich amber exude from tamarisk bark.   55
Let screech owls contend with swans. Let Tityrus
be Orpheus of the woods, Arion among the dolphins—
    Begin with me, my flute, the verses of Maenalus.
Let ocean cover everything. Farewell woods:
from my lofty lookout on the hills I'll plunge headlong   60
into the waves; let Nysa have this, my gift at death.
    Leave off now, my flute, the verses of Maenalus.
This was Damon's song. What Alphesiboeus replied
tell, Pierides. We can't do everything.
A.   Bring water. With supple fillets girt the altars here.   65
Burn the resinous bundles and masculine frankincense

that I may try to turn from sanity the sense
of my betrothed. Nothing is lacking here but the spells.
    Bring from the city, my magic songs, bring Daphnis home.
Spells can even draw the moon down from the sky.   70
With spells did Circe transform the companions of Odysseus.
By spells the chilly snake in the meadows is burst apart.
    Bring from the city, my magic songs, bring Daphnis home.
First, three threads of triple-colored strands I wind
around, and three times around these altars I draw   75
your effigy. In the odd number god delights.
    Bring from the city, my magic songs, bring Daphnis home.
Amaryllis, knot three times the triple-colored strands.
Amaryllis, knot them and say, "The bonds of Venus I knot."
    Bring from the city, my magic songs, bring Daphnis home.   80
As this clay hardens and this wax liquifies
in the same fire, so may Daphnis for love of me.
Scatter the barley and burn the brittle bay with pitch.
Wicked Daphnis burns me; I for Daphnis this bay.
    Bring from the city, my magic songs, bring Daphnis home.   85
Such be Daphnis's love as when a heifer, weary
from seeking the young bull through forests and deep groves,
sinks upon the green sedge beside a brook,
despairing, nor does she notice the late hour of night.
May love like this take him and I not care to heal.   90
    Bring from the city, my magic songs, bring Daphnis home.
This clothing, formerly his, that traitor left to me,
dear pledges of himself. Now I, on the doorstep itself
commit them to you, O earth. These pledges owe me Daphnis.
    Bring from the city, my magic songs, bring Daphnis home.   95
These poisons, these herbs, gathered in Pontus, Moeris himself
gave to me. In Pontus they grow abundantly.
I've often seen with these Moeris become a wolf
and hide in the woods, often call souls from the depths of the grave,
and charm the harvests away from the fields where they
    were sown.   100

Bring from the city, my magic songs, bring Daphnis home.
Bring ashes and cast them out of doors across your head
into the flowing stream and don't look back. With these
I'll get at Daphnis. He cares for neither gods nor songs.

Bring from the city, my magic songs, bring Daphnis home.   105
Look, the ash itself of its own accord has caught
the altar with flickering flame before I can fetch it.
May it be good! It's something: in the doorway Hylax barks.
Dare I believe it? Or do lovers create their dreams?

Cease, my magic songs; from the city Daphnis comes.   110

ECLOGUE IX

Lycidas, Moeris

L. Moeris, where do you go? Is it to town perhaps?
M. O Lycidas, that we have lived for this, that what
    we never feared, a stranger possess our little field
    and say, "These are mine. Be off, tenants of old!"
    Undone and sorrowing, since fortune reverses all,   5
    we drive these kids for him (and may it do him no good!).
L. Surely I had heard that where the hills begin
    to withdraw and lower their ridge with gentle slope
    to water and ancient beeches with broken branches atop—
    that all this your Menalcas had saved with his songs.   10
M. You'd heard, and so the story went, but, Lycidas,
    our songs are worth as much among the weapons of Mars
    as Chaonian doves, they say, before the eagle's flight.
    Had not a crow from the hollow tree at my left hand
    admonished me to cut short my fresh suit,   15
    neither your Moeris nor Menalcas himself would live.
L. Alas, can such wickedness be anyone's?
    Alas for your comfort nearly lost to us with you,
    Menalcas! Who would sing the nymphs—who would strew
    the earth with flowering herbs or canopy the springs   20
    with green shade—or the songs I lately picked up from you
    when you were on your way to darling Amaryllis?
    "Tityrus, until I return, pasture the goats
    (I won't be long) and drive them to drink and take care
    not to cross the billy goat—he butts with his horn."   25
M. Rather these, which unfinished, he sang to Varus:
    "Varus, your name, if only our Mantua survive,
    Mantua, a neighbor too near to wretched Cremona,
    singing swans shall carry on high to the very stars."

L.   So may your swarms avoid the yews of Corsica.   30
     So may your cattle fed on clover distend their teats.
     Begin with what you have. The Pierides have made
     me a poet too, and I have songs as well.
     Shepherds call me a bard, but them I can't believe.
     Not yet do I think I sing as well as Varius   35
     or Cinna—a goose that cackles among the shrilling swans.

M. Lycidas, this is what I silently ponder myself:
     whether I can remember: it's no unworthy song.
     "Come here, O Galataea. What sport is there in the waves?
     Here is blushing spring. Here the earth around   40
     the streams puts flowers forth. Here the silvery poplar
     covers the cave and pliant vines weave their shade.
     Come here and let the furious billows beat on the shore."

L.   What about the song I heard you singing beneath
     the night sky? I remember the notes if I had the words: 45
     "Daphnis, why do you gaze at the ancient constellations
     as they rise? The star of Caesar, Dione's child,
     has appeared, the star by which the crops should rejoice in fruit
     and the grape take color upon the sunny hills. Daphnis,
     engraft your pears. Your children's children shall pluck
        the fruit."   50

M. Time bears all away; the mind as well. As a boy
     I recall spending the long sunlit days in song.
     Now I've forgotten so many songs. Moeris too
     loses his voice. The wolves have caught first sight of him.
     But Menalcas will recite them often enough to you.   55

L.   With talking you put off fulfillment of our desire.
     Now look, all the sea is smooth and still, and see,
     all the breath of murmuring breezes has died away.
     Just from here is half our way, for Bianor's tomb
     begins to show. Here where farmers strip the leaves   60
     grown too dense, here, Moeris, let us sing.
     Here put down your kids. Still we'll reach the town.
     Or if we fear that rain will fall before the night,

we can sing as we go (the road will tire us less).
That we sing as we go, I'll take this bundle from you.   65
M. No more, my boy. Let us do the task at hand.
When Menalcas comes, we'll better sing his songs.

ECLOGUE X

Arethusa, my Muse, allow to me this final work:
I must sing to my Gallus a little song, which Lycoris herself
might read. Who would deny to Gallus such a song?
So that when you slip beneath Sicilian waves,
bitter Doris not mingle her ocean waves with yours,   5
begin: Let us tell of Gallus's troubled loves
while the flat-nosed she-goats crop the tender brush,
nor do we sing to the deaf; the forests echo all.
    What groves, what mountain pastures kept you, naiad girls,
when Gallus was perishing of unrequited love?   10
For neither the ridges of Parnassus nor of Pindus
caused your delay nor did Aonian Aganippe.
Even the laurels, even the tamarisks wept for him,
even pine-covered Maenalus wept as he lay beneath
a lonely cliff, and the rocks of chill Lycaeus wept.   15
Sheep stand round about, unashamed of us,
nor do you, poet divine, repent of your flock.
Even comely Adonis pastured his sheep at the stream.
The shepherd came, and with slower pace the swineherds came.
Menalcas, dripping from the winter acorns, came.   20
All ask, "Whence that love of yours?" Apollo came.
"Gallus, why this madness?" he said. "Lycoris, your love,
has followed another through snows and camps bristling with arms."
Silvanus came, crowned with rustic ornament,
tossing his flowing fennel and large lilies about.   25
Pan, the god of Arcadia, came, whom we have seen
stained red with vermilion and crimson elderberries.
He said, "Enough! Love cares not for such. Cruel,
neither is he sated with tears nor grass with brooks
nor bees with clover nor nanny goats with leafy sprays."   30
But sadly he said, "Still, Arcadians, you will sing
these songs to your hills. Arcadians alone are skilled to sing.

How softly my bones would rest if only your pipe
should someday tell of my loves. Would that I had been
one of yours, a shepherd of your flock or a dresser   35
of the ripe grape. Surely Amyntas or Phyllis then
or whoever my passion was (what if Amyntas be
swarthy? Violets are dark and blueberries too)
would lie among the willows beneath the pliant vine
with me. Phyllis would gather garlands for me, Amyntas sing.   40
Here are chilly springs, here the soft meadows,
Lycoris, here the wood. Here with time itself
I'd waste away with you. Now a mad love
keeps me in arms of Mars amid his weapons with foes
opposed. You, far from your native land (I wish   45
that I didn't believe it!) look upon the Alpine snows
and frosts of the Rhine, without me, alone. May the frosts not bite!
And, oh, may the piercing ice not cut your delicate feet!
I will go and the songs that I composed in verse
of Chalcis I'll set for a Sicilian shepherd's pipe.   50
I'm resolved in the woods to endure among the caves
of wild beasts and to cut my loves on tender trees.
As those trees grow, so also you will grow, my loves.
Meanwhile I will wander over Maenalus
with nymphs and hunt the fierce wild boars. Nor will frost   55
prevent me from encircling Parthenian groves with hounds.
Now I seem to go among rocks and echoing groves
and thrill to whirl Cydonian shafts from Parthian bow—
as though this could be the healing of my madness
or that god learn compassion for the woes of men.   60
Now neither hamadryads again nor songs themselves
give pleasure to us. Forests yourselves, again withdraw.
Our labors can't change him. Neither if we drink
of Hebrus amid the frosts nor endure the snows
of stormy winter, nor if when the dying bark parches   65
upon the lofty elm we drive Ethiopian sheep
beneath Cancer. Love conquers all. Let us yield too."

This will be enough, goddesses of Pieria,
for your poet to sing while he sits and weaves a basket of
slender mallow. You'll make this song precious for Gallus,   70
Gallus for whom my love grows as much by the hour
as the green alder shoots up when spring is ripening.
Let us get up. The shade is apt to be harmful to singers.
The shade of the juniper harms, and shade harms the crops.
Go home, my well-fed goats, now go, for Hesperus comes.   75

NOTES

The line numbers in the notes refer to my translation rather than to the Latin text. My translation is almost but not quite line for line. Cross-references to other notes cite the eclogue number and line number (I.6n meaning, for example, the note to the sixth line of *Eclogue I*).

ECLOGUE I

1 **Tityrus.** A slave who has at last bought his freedom and has been successful in his plea to Octavian to restore to him the land that had been allotted to Antony's soldiers. See the Introduction. The name is Greek and is taken from Theocritus.

5 **Amaryllis.** A girl, probably a slave. The name is taken from Theocritus.

6 **Meliboeus.** A Roman citizen who has lost his lands to the confiscations and is forced to go into exile. The name is Greek but is not from Theocritus.

7 **He'll always be a god to me** refers to the young Octavian. See the Introduction.

30 **Galataea.** In Theocritus an ocean nymph wooed by the Cyclops but here presumably another slave girl.

55 **Hyblaean.** Refers to the city Megara Hyblaea, slightly north of Syracuse in Sicily, which was known for its excellent honey.

63 **Parthian.** A native of Parthia, a country of Asia southeast of the Caspian Sea. The Parthians were a notoriously warlike people whose tactics included surrounding the enemy and pouring in upon them a shower of darts and then fleeing while shooting their arrows backward upon the enemy. Their empire extended over Asia from the Euphrates to the Indus, from the Indian Ocean possibly to the Oxus River. Antony campaigned unsuccessfully against the Parthians in 36 B.C.

63 **Arar.** A river of Germany.

64 **Babylonian Tigris.** One of the great rivers of Babylonia (modern Iraq). "Babylonian" does not appear in the Latin text. I added it for the sake of the meter.

67 **Scythia.** A region of western Asia north of the Black and Caspian Seas.

67 **Oaxes.** Possibly the river Oxus in central Asia, now the Amu-Dar'ya, which flows into the Aral Sea, "a remote and fabulous river of which V. can have had only the vaguest notion" (W. Clausen, *A Commentary on Vergil, Eclogues* [Oxford, 1994], 56 on 65).

ECLOGUE II

This eclogue is modeled after Theocritus's *Idyll XI,* in which the grotesque Cyclops woos the lovely sea nymph Galataea. Here a simple shepherd laments his love for a slave boy who is being kept by their common master.

1 **Corydon.** A shepherd. In Theocritus, *Idyll IV,* the name belongs to a cowherd.

6 **Alexis.** A slave boy. Alexis is a traditional name for a catamite.

15 **Amaryllis.** See I.5n.

16 **Menalcas.** Evidently a boy with whom Corydon was once in love. The name is taken from Theocritus, *Idyll VIII.*

24 **Amphion of Dirce.** Amphion was a son of Zeus and Antiope, reared by shepherds and famous for his playing of the lyre. He was said to have built the walls of Thebes with his music: the stones moved into place as he played. Dirce was a fountain near Thebes, in central Greece.

25 **Actaean Aracynthus.** Actaean refers to Attica, in central Greece. Vergil seems to think that the mountain Aracynthus was located on the border between Attica and Boeotia to the north, but we know of no mountain of that name in that location. There was a Mount Aracynthus in Acarnania, in western Greece.

28 **Daphnis.** A name taken from Theocritus and used in Vergil for an idealized shepherd, beloved by Pan. In Theocritus he is a cowherd. In *Idyll I,* he is dying of an unnamed love; in *Idyll VII,* of love for a girl named Xenea.

32 **Pan.** A Greek god of shepherds and flocks, usually a son of Hermes. He originally belonged to Arcadia, of the Peloponnesus, in southern Greece. He invented the shepherd's pipe. In art he is often portrayed as snub-nosed, horned, and with goat's feet.

36 **Amyntas.** In Theocritus, *Idyll VII*, a real person but in Vergil a fictional shepherd.

38 **Damoetas.** Also a fictional person. In Theocritus, *Idyll VI*, he impersonates the Cyclops.

47 **naiad.** A nymph of fresh water: rivers, springs, lakes, and brooks.

63 **Paris of Troy.** The son of Priam and Hecuba, who stole Helen and thus caused the Trojan War. He was brought up as a shepherd on Mount Ida in Asia Minor.

63 **Pallas Athene.** The Greek goddess of wisdom and war. She is often referred to as guardian of the city, especially of Athens.

ECLOGUE III

In this eclogue, two shepherds, Menalcas and Damoetas, meet and agree to engage in a singing contest. After deciding what each shall wager, they invite Palaemon, who is passing by, to be their judge. The poem is modeled after Theocritus, *Idylls IV* and *V*.

1 **Damoetas.** The name is taken from Theocritus, *Idyll VI*. The character is imaginary.

1 **Meliboeus.** See I.6n.

2 **Aegon.** Damoetas's master.

4 **Neaera.** A name long associated with easy virtue.

10 **Micon.** The name is taken from Theocritus, *Idyll IV*.

14 **Menalcas.** See II.16n.

16 **Damon.** A fictional character.

17 **Lycisca.** The name properly belongs to a mongrel bitch.

36 **Alcimedon.** A fictional artist.

39 **Conon.** A Samian astronomer and mathematician who lived and worked in Alexandria, Egypt.

45 **Orpheus.** A legendary musician of Thrace, in northern Greece, who accompanied the Argonauts. Given the lyre by Apollo and taught by the Muses, he charmed the wild beasts, trees, and rocks upon Olympus to follow him.

49 **Palaemon.** Another fictional character.

59 **Jove.** Jupiter, the king of the gods.

61 **Phoebus.** Apollo. See below, 103n.

66 **Delia.** A slave name.

75 **Phyllis.** A fictional girl.

75 **Iollas.** A non-Theocritean name. In *Eclogue II* he was the shepherd's master.

83 **Pollio.** C. Asinius Pollio. He had supported Caesar and later Antony, and in 41 B.C. the latter appointed him legate of Cisalpine Gaul (northern Italy). It may have been then that he became acquainted with Vergil and urged him to try his hand at pastoral poetry. He was a patron of poets and himself a poet. See also the Introduction.

84 **Pierides.** The Muses, so named from their early home, Pieria, on the southeast coast of Macedonia, in northern Greece.

89 **Bavius** and **Maevius,** two real poets of whom we know nothing further.

103 **Apollo.** God of music and light.

ECLOGUE IV

This eclogue is not truly a pastoral. That is why Vergil suggests to the **Sicilian Muses** (1) that he sing a somewhat nobler theme, the consulship in 40 B.C. of his patron C. Asinius **Pollio** (12; see the Introduction and III.83n). The Sicilian Muses are those of the Sicilian poet Theocritus, many of whose lines Vergil echoes in his own pastoral poems. The poem celebrates the Pact of Brundisium, negotiated by Pollio, which promised at least a respite from the civil wars from which Rome had suffered for nearly a century.

The prophecies that Vergil utters in this eclogue come from several sources and comprise no complete system. The **Cumaean Sybil** (4) was a prophetess at Cumae on the western coast of Italy. The Sybilline books probably copied an Etruscan theory of a succession of ten *saecula*, that is periods of 110 years, the last of which would be under the rule of Apollo and so especially happy. The **Maiden** (6) is Justice, and this involves quite another source. She appears in the same context in the Greek poet Aratus's *Phaenomena*. Here Vergil, like Aratus, calls upon the Hesiodic concept of the Golden, Silver, Bronze, and Iron Ages. (Hesiod inserted an Age of Heroes between the Bronze and Iron Ages.) In the Golden Age, before the moral decline of man, **Saturn** (6) — an old Roman deity of planting, later identified with the Greek Cronus, father of Zeus—reigned. Vergil states that with Pollio's consulate and the birth of the unnamed child a new Golden Age, that is, a new age of Saturn, will begin. **Lucina** (10), often identified with Diana, is the goddess of childbirth.

The mighty sequence of ages (5) may also refer to the astronomical theory of the *magnus annus* (great year), the great cycle completed when the heavenly bodies were in the same position they had been in at the time of creation. It was then that a new era would begin. Stoic philosophy identified the *magnus annus* with the period between "the successive conflagrations that dissolve the universe into its original 'creative fire'" (R. Coleman, *Vergil, Eclogues* [Cambridge, 1977], 130 on 5).

Who, scholars have wondered over the centuries, is the **child** (8)? Several possibilities have been suggested. (1) Pollio is said by an ancient source to have had two sons, Saloninus and Asinius Gallus. We have no other evidence that Saloninus actually lived, but Asinius Gallus, born in 41 B.C., a year before the notional date of this poem, and consul in 8 B.C., claimed that the eclogue had been written about him. Since the poem is obviously a tribute to his father, this seems to me not unlikely. (2) Mark Antony and Cleopatra had twins, possibly in 40 B.C., but Romans were so outraged by Antony's liaison with Cleopatra that it is unlikely Vergil could be referring to their children. (3) The Pact of Brundisium was sealed with a marriage between Antony and Octavia, Octavian's sister, in 40 B.C., but they did not in fact have a child. (4) Octavian and Scribonia were married in 40 B.C., but the child they produced was a girl. (5) For centuries, Christians thought the eclogue a prediction of the birth of Christ. Although Vergil may have been aware of the Messianic literature of the East, the poem itself is so steeped in the beliefs and imagery of the Greek and Roman worlds that there is no need to accept such an interpretation.

Eclogue IV goes on to say that not until the baby has become a man will the Golden Age truly begin. The Golden Age literature of Greece and so of Rome insisted that because of man's iniquity he was forced to sail dangerous seas in search of livelihood, to labor in fields for his food, and to fortify his towns with walls. In the Golden Age all this will change. First, however, men will have to pay for **traces of their old iniquity** (31).

34 **Tiphys** was helmsman of the **Argo**, the ship in which Jason sailed after the golden fleece.

36 **Achilles** was the chief hero of the great war the Greeks waged against **Troy**, the city upon the Hellespont in Asia Minor.

46 The **Fates** were Clotho, Lachesis, and Atropos. They spun out and cut off the destinies of men.

55 **Thracian Orpheus.** See III.45n.

56 **Linus.** A legendary poet, whom Hesiod called "learned in every kind of wisdom." He is especially associated with dirges.

57 **Calliope.** The Muse of epic poetry or of poetry in general. Mother of Orpheus. In some accounts both Linus and Orpheus were sons of Calliope and Apollo.

58 **Pan.** See II.32n.

58 **Arcadia.** A district of the Peloponnesus, in southern Greece. It is commonly the setting for pastoral poetry.

ECLOGUE V

In this eclogue, two shepherds meet and agree to a singing contest. Mopsus, the younger, sings of the death of Daphnis. Menalcas, the elder, sings of Daphnis's deification. There are echoes throughout of Theocritus, *Idylls I, VI, VII,* and *VIII,* and of pseudo-Moschus's *Lament for Bion,* but the erotic element of *Idyll I* in which Daphnis pines away for a mysterious love, is here suppressed. The poem has often been taken as a reference to the apotheosis of Julius Caesar, who was assassinated in March, 44 B.C. A comet that appeared in the northern skies four months later was believed to symbolize his assumption into heaven. In *Eclogue IX* Daphnis looks upon "Caesar's star" as a portent of rural prosperity. The triumvirs apparently granted divine honors to Caesar in 43 B.C., and on July 12, 42 B.C., his birthday was celebrated with religious rites and the month of Quintilis named July in his honor. It is therefore not unlikely that *Eclogue V* does obliquely refer to the presumed deification of Julius Caesar.

1 **Mopsus.** The name does not appear in pastoral before Vergil.

4 **Menalcas.** See II.16n.

8 **Amyntas.** See II.36n.

11 **Phyllis.** See III.75n.

11 **Alcon.** A Greek name found only here in Vergil.

11 **Codrus.** A fictional person.

20 **Daphnis.** See II.28n.

27 **Punic.** Carthaginian, that is, of Carthage, the city in North Africa.

28 **Armenian.** Of Armenia, a country of the Near East. Armenian tigers were proverbially fierce. Bacchus is said to have yoked them to his chariot. Critics have sometimes seen this as a reference to Julius Caesar as a restorer of peace and order after the civil wars.

30 **Bacchic revelers.** Worshipers of Dionysus, the god of wine. Daphnis is here presented as having introduced the worship of Dionysus to shepherds.

34 **Fates.** See IV.46n.

35 **Pales.** An Italian deity of flocks and herds.

35 **Apollo.** See III.103n.

55 **Stimichon.** An imaginary person. The name is not attested before Vergil.

57 **Olympus.** The mountain in northern Greece said to be the home of the gods.

60 **dryad.** A wood nymph.

73 **Ariusian.** An especially fine wine from a region on the northwestern coast of Chios, an island of the Aegean. The best Greek wines came from Chios.

74 **Damoetas.** See II.38n.

74 **Lyctian Aegon.** Lyctian means Cretan, that is, of the island Crete in the Mediterranean. Aegon is an imaginary person.

75 **Alphesiboeus.** An imaginary person whose name is a Greek adjective used originally of girls who brought cattle to their parents as wedding presents from their suitors. Later it meant "cattle-fattening." A feminine form occurs as a name in Greek legend, but the masculine form seems to be Vergil's invention.

81 **Bacchus.** A name of Dionysus, the god of wine.

81 **Ceres.** The goddess of grain.

93 **Antigenes.** In Theocritus, *Idyll VII*, the name of a real person but in Vergil a purely fictional character.

This eclogue does not reflect Theocritean pastoral. Critics have seen in it, rather, the influence of Callimachus, another Hellenistic poet who eschewed epic for lighter genres. It was, in fact, he who said, "a big book is a big evil." The subjects of Silenus's songs are thought to be those suitable for the Roman neoteric (i.e., their own Alexandrian movement) poetry, and one critic has ingeniously argued that they are a list of the poems of Gallus, a friend and fellow poet of Vergil (see below, 65n). Since none of Gallus's works has survived, it is impossible to prove this. Alfenus **Varus** (6), to whom the poem is dedicated, had replaced Pollio in Cisalpine Gaul and became in his turn a patron of Vergil. He, together with Gallus, seems also to have helped Vergil recover his farm. Lines 32–41, in which Silenus tells of the creation, are vaguely Lucretian in tone, but the details do not match any fixed philosophy. (Lucretius was a Roman poet, much admired by Vergil, who wrote a long poem, *On the Nature of Things*, propounding the philosophy of the Greek thinker Epicurus.)

1 **Syracusan verse.** Poetry like that of Theocritus, i.e., pastoral.

2 **Thalia.** The Muse of comedy and of pastoral poetry.

3 **Cynthius.** Apollo.

4 **Tityrus.** See I.1n.

6 **Varus.** See above, introductory note to this eclogue.

12 **Phoebus.** Apollo.

13–14 **Mnasyllus and Chromis.** Imaginary characters.

14 **Silenus.** A satyr, companion of Bacchus, the god of wine. He is usually portrayed as bald, snub-nosed, and lascivious. He was also an inspired prophet and, when drunk or asleep, in the power of mortals, who by entangling him in chains of flowers could compel him to sing or prophesy.

30 **Parnassian rock.** Mount Parnassus in Phocis, in central Greece, sacred to Apollo and the Muses.

31 **Rhodope.** A mountain in Thrace, in northern Greece, home of Orpheus.

31 **Ismarus.** Also a mountain in Thrace.

31 **Orpheus.** See III.45n.

42 **Pyrrha.** Wife of Deucalion, king of Thessaly, in northern Greece. Zeus

saved them while destroying the rest of mankind by a flood. They repeopled the earth by throwing stones behind their backs.

42–43 **reign of Saturn.** The Golden Age. See introductory note to *Eclogue IV.*

43 **Caucasian vultures.** The creatures who fed on Prometheus's liver when he was chained to a mountain in the Caucasus in Asia. Vergil's plural is unusual.

43 **Prometheus's theft.** He stole fire from heaven for mankind—the act for which he was punished by Zeus by being chained to a mountain.

44 **Hylas.** A beautiful boy who went with Hercules on the expedition of the Argonauts in quest of the golden fleece. While he was drawing water from a well, the nymphs who lived there fell in love with him and drew him down to live with them.

46 **Pasiphaë.** Wife of King Minos of Crete. She fell in love with a bull and so gave birth to the Minotaur, a creature half man and half bull. She was also the mother of Ariadne and Phaedra.

49 **Proteus's daughters.** Proteus was a king of Argos in the Peloponnesus, in southern Greece. His daughters were punished with madness either for despising Dionysus (Bacchus) or for daring to compare themselves in beauty with Hera (Juno) and imagined themselves to be cows.

57 **Dictaean.** Cretan, i.e., of Crete, the large Greek island in the Mediterranean Sea. From the mountain Dicte there, on which Jupiter was reared.

60 **Gortynian.** Also Cretan. From the chief town of the island, Gortyna.

62 **Hesperides.** Daughters of the Evening. They lived on an island in the extreme west in a garden with golden apples guarded by a dragon.

63 **Phaethon.** "Shining One." A son of Helios, the sun. He tried to drive his father's chariot, but he was unable to restrain the horses, and they came so close to the earth that they almost set it on fire. Zeus (Jupiter) then struck him with lightning and hurled him down into the river Eridanus, a legendary river later identified with the Po in Italy. His sisters, who had helped him yoke the horses, were changed into poplars or—as here—into alders and their tears into amber.

65 **Gallus.** C. Cornelius Gallus, the Roman poet who befriended Vergil. He was born in Gaul but early in life went to Italy, where he rose to prominence under Julius Caesar and Augustus. Augustus appointed him prefect of Egypt. He somehow displeased the emperor, and the Senate sent

him into exile. He committed suicide in 26 B.C. The poet Ovid considered him the greatest of the elegiac poets. All that is left of his work is one half line.

66 **Permessus.** A river in Boeotia, in central Greece, sacred to the Muses. It rose on Mount Helicon and flowed into the Copaic Lake.

66 **Aonian.** Boeotian.

68 **Linus.** See IV.56n.

71 **Ascraean elder.** Hesiod, the early Greek poet who was born in Ascra, a small town of Boeotia. He wrote the *Theogony* and *Works and Days*.

73 **Grynaean grove.** Grynia was a town in Asia Minor with a temple and oracle of Apollo.

75 **Nisus's Scylla.** Vergil has here confused two stories. Scylla and Charybdis are two rocks between Sicily and Italy. In Homer, Scylla is a monster that barks like a dog and has twelve feet, as well as six long necks and heads, each with three rows of sharp teeth. Here she is portrayed as being girt with barking dogs. Charybdis was the whirlpool opposite, which sucked down sailors. Scylla, the daughter of Nisus, king of Megara in central Greece, was quite another person. She fell in love with Minos of Crete when he was besieging her father's city and so pulled out the purple (or, in some versions of her story, golden) lock on which his life depended. Nisus died and Minos took the city. In disgust, Minos fastened Scylla to the poop of his ship and drowned her. In other versions, Nisus, who had been changed into a sea eagle, swooped down on her, whereupon she was changed into either a fish or a bird called Ciris.

77 **Dulichium.** An island in the Ionian Sea. It was part of Ulysses's (i.e., Odysseus's) kingdom.

79 **Tereus.** Married Procne, daughter of Pandion, king of Attica, in central Greece. Later he shut her away, claiming that she was dead, and married her sister **Philomela** (80). When Philomela learned the truth, she punished Tereus by killing her son Itys and serving him up to his father for a meal. The two women fled, but Tereus pursued them. Procne was then, in answer to her prayer, changed into a nightingale. Tereus was changed into a hoopoe. For another version of the story, see Ovid, *Metamorphoses* VI.430 ff.

83 **Eurotas.** A river of Lacedaemonia in the Peloponnesus, in southern Greece.

ECLOGUE VII

This is another singing contest in the Theocritean manner. Meliboeus recalls it and at the end states that Corydon vanquished Thyrsis. Critics have wasted centuries wondering why.

5 **Arcadian.** Of Arcadia. See IV.58n.

12 **Mincius.** A river near Mantua, in northern Italy. Now the Mincio.

21 **Libethran.** Of Libethra, a spring of Thessaly, in northern Greece, sacred to the Muses.

33 **Priapus.** Son of Dionysus and Aphrodite, god of fruitfulness and protector of flocks of sheep and goats, of bees, and of all garden produce. He was usually represented as ithyphallic.

37 **Nereid.** A sea nymph.

38 **Hybla.** See I.55n.

41 **Sardinian grass.** The "Sardinian herb" was said to have been a kind of ranunculus so bitter that it caused a "sardonic smile." Sardinian honey was notoriously bitter.

51 **Boreas.** The North Wind.

58 **Liber.** An old Italian deity presiding over agriculture. He later became identified with Bacchus, the god of wine.

60 **Jupiter.** The same as Jove, king of the gods.

61 **Alcides.** Hercules, as the grandson of Alcaeus.

61 **Iacchus.** A name of Bacchus.

62 **Venus.** The goddess of love.

ECLOGUE VIII

This eclogue is modeled upon two Theocritean idylls. Damon's song borrows the general idea and some details from *Idyll III*. Alphesiboeus's song is modeled upon *Idyll II*, in which a woman, with the help of her servant, works magic spells to bring her delinquent lover home.

It had long been assumed that *Eclogue VIII* was dedicated to Pollio, for the reference to the buskin of Sophocles must, critics supposed, refer to his writing of tragedy. The recent argument against such an identification is that Pollio would not have had reason at this date to be sailing past the Timavus or along the Illyrian coast. Octavian, on the other hand, would have had good reason to do so. In 35 B.C. he had conduct-ed campaigns in northern Dalmatia in the general area of the Timavus River. But did he write tragedy? An ancient source tells us that he did begin to compose an *Ajax* but abandoned the enterprise, remarking, when asked about his progress, that Ajax had fallen upon his sponge (Clausen, 231–36). The dedication to Pollio still seems to me the more likely.

1 **Damon.** The name of a herdsman in *Eclogue III*.

1 **Alphesiboeus.** See V.75n.

6 **rocks of mighty Timavus.** The Timavus is a river (now the Timavo) that flows into the Adriatic Sea. Sixteen miles from its source it becomes sub-terranean; it emerges after eighteen miles in the form of many springs that flow together to form the river again. Vergil exaggerates the size of the river, and the rocks may well have been his invention.

7 **Illyrian waters.** The waters off Illyricum, a district on the Adriatic coast, opposite the eastern coast of Italy. Its coast was particularly dangerous.

10 **buskin of Sophocles.** The buskin was the high boot worn by actors of Greek tragedy and so refers here to Pollio's (or Octavian's?) writing of tragedy.

17 **Lucifer.** The morning star, that is, the planet Venus.

21 **Maenalus.** A mountain of Arcadia in the Peloponnesus, in southern Greece, sacred to Pan. "Verses of Maenalus" means pastoral poetry.

24 **Pan.** See II.32n.

26 **Mopsus.** The younger singer in *Eclogue V.*

26 **Nysa.** A woman given in marriage to Mopsus.

31 **Vesper.** The evening star, which is the same as the morning star, that is, the planet Venus.

31 **Oeta.** A mountain in Thessaly, in northern Greece.

45 **Tmaros.** A mountain range in Epirus, in western Greece. The famous oracle of Dodona was located in the valley beside it.

45 **Rhodope.** See VI.31n.

45 **Garamants.** Tribesmen of the eastern Sahara in Africa.

48–49 **Savage Love taught the mother to spatter her hands with children's blood.** A reference to Medea, who murdered her two children to spite her husband, Jason, because he intended to leave her for another woman.

56 **Tityrus.** See I.1n.

57 **Orpheus.** See III.45n.

57 **Arion.** Poet and lyre player at the court of Periander in Corinth, in central Greece, about 625 B.C. When Corinthian sailors plotted to rob him of treasures he had won at a musical contest, he played the lyre, invoking the gods to save him, and then jumped overboard. One of the dolphins that he had charmed with his song carried him on its back safely back to Corinth, where he told all to Periander.

64 **Pierides.** See III.84n.

69 **Daphnis.** See II.28n.

71 **Odysseus.** The hero of Homer's *Odyssey*; he spent ten years wandering over the seas on his way home from Troy to Ithaca and his wife Penelope.

78 **Amaryllis.** See I.5n.

96 **Pontus.** A district of Asia Minor between Bithynia and Armenia, known for its poisons, especially aconite. Vergil may, however, mean Colchis, Medea's home, at the eastern end of the Black Sea (Clausen, 263).

96 **Moeris.** The name of a dispossessed farmer in *Eclogue IX*. The name is non-Theocritean. Here, apparently, he is a werewolf.

108 **Hylax.** The name of a dog. It seems to mean "Barker."

ECLOGUE IX

In this eclogue, two shepherds, Lycidas and Moeris, meet. Moeris has apparently been turned off his land or is at least only a tenant farmer to the new owner. Lycidas is surprised, for he had supposed that Menalcas had saved the lands in the area with his songs. Critics have—on the basis of this statement and lines 86–87 (89–90 in my translation) of *Eclogue V*, where Vergil quotes himself—sometimes identified Menalcas with Vergil. So specific an identification is surely mistaken, but there can be no doubt that Vergil in this eclogue is referring to the confiscations that were taking place in the the district around Mantua. In this poem however, the tone is sadder than in *Eclogue I*, which dealt with the same theme. The emphasis is upon the loss of inspiration for song rather than upon the loss of land in itself. There are Theocritean echoes throughout, especially of *Idylls VII* and *XI*, but the ambience is nevertheless Italian. The poem has often been taken as an appeal to Varus to restore Vergil's father's farm to him.

1 **Moeris.** The name of the werewolf in *Eclogue VIII*. Here, however, a dispossessed farmer.

2 **Lycidas.** In Theocritus, *Idyll VII*, he is the mysterious Pan-like goatherd, but here he seems to be just an idealized shepherd-poet.

10 **Menalcas.** See II.16n. and the introductory note to this eclogue.

12 **Mars.** The god of war.

13 **Chaonian doves.** The oracular doves or dove-priestesses of Dodona at the famous oracle of Zeus in Thresprotia, in western Greece.

23 **Tityrus.** See I.1n. These lines (23–25 in my translation) are taken from Theocritus, *Idyll III*.3–5.

26 **Varus.** L. Alfenus Varus. He was one of those responsible for redistributing the lands around Mantua and may also have been one of those who intervened with Octavian on Vergil's behalf (see the Introduction). The eclogue has often been taken as an appeal to Varus and thought therefore to be earlier in date of composition than *Eclogue I*.

27 **Mantua.** A town of Cisalpine Gaul (northern Italy) near Vergil's birthplace of Andes.

28 **Cremona.** Another town of Cisalpine Gaul near Mantua.

30 **Corsica.** An island in the Mediterranean west of Italy. Corsican honey was, like Sardinian, very bitter, and the island's yews were harmful to bees.

32 **Pierides.** See III.84n.

35 **Varius.** L. Varius Rufus, a friend of Vergil and like him an early member of the circle of Maecenas, Octavian's wealthy minister who was a patron of both Horace and Vergil. Vergil, Varius, and Plotius Tucca all accompanied Horace on the famous Journey to Brundisium (Horace, *Satire I*). Varius and Plotius Tucca were to be the editors of the *Aeneid* after Vergil's death. Varius himself had a reputation as an epic poet and tragedian. He produced a *Thyestes* on the occasion of Octavian's triple triumph in 29 B.C.

36 **Cinna.** L. Helvius Cinna, an epic poet who was murdered by the mob after Julius Caesar's assassination when he was mistaken for the conspirator Cornelius Cinna.

39 **Galataea.** These lines are in imitation of Theocritus, *Idyll XI*.19, where

the Cyclops courts the sea nymph Galataea. Here Galataea is the sea nymph and not, as in *Eclogue I*, an ordinary girl.

47 **Caesar, Dione's child.** This is again a reference to the comet that appeared shortly after the assassination of Julius Caesar and was supposed to herald his assumption into heaven. The Julian family claimed descent from Iulus, son of Aeneas, grandson of Venus, whose mother was Dione.

54 **The wolves have caught first sight of him.** Superstition held that if a wolf saw a man before the man saw it, the man would lose his voice (T. E. Page, *P. Vergili Maronis: Bucolica et Georgica* [London, 1931], 171 on 54).

59 **Bianor's tomb.** This is taken from Theocritus, *Idyll VII*.10–11, where the tomb of Brasilas was a landmark on the Aegean island of Cos. Bianor himself is otherwise unknown. His tomb is probably fictional.

ECLOGUE X

Vergil composed this "last" eclogue for his friend and fellow poet Gallus, who is in Arcadia lamenting his lost Lycoris. She has apparently deserted him for a soldier who is campaigning in some northern clime. The poem is modeled in part on Theocritus, *Idyll I*, in which cowherds, shepherds, and goatherds as well as animals of the wild come to lament Daphnis, who is dying of love.

1 **Arethusa.** An Arcadian nymph who was pursued by the river god Alpheus. Diana turned her into a river that flowed under the Ionian Sea and emerged as a freshwater spring on the island Ortygia in the harbor of Syracuse, Sicily. Here Vergil invokes her as a Muse of pastoral poetry, presumably in honor of Theocritus, the Sicilian inventor of the genre.

2 **Gallus.** See introductory note to *Eclogue VI* and VI.65.

2 **Lycoris.** A famous actress whose stage name was Cytheris and whose real name, as a freedwoman of Volumnus Eutrapelus, was Volumnia. She has apparently deserted Gallus, perhaps for an officer in the service of Agrippa, who led an expedition across the Rhine and into Gaul in 37 B.C. Gallus is represented as being both on military service elsewhere and in an idealized Arcadia.

4 **Sicilian waves.** Refers to the story told above, 1n.

5 **bitter Doris.** Doris, a sea nymph, here stands for the salt water of the ocean as opposed to Arethusa's fresh water.

9 **naiad.** See II.47n.

11 **Parnassus.** See VI.30n.

11 **Pindus.** A mountain range dividing Thessaly from Epirus in northwestern Greece.

12 **Aonian Aganippe.** Aonian means Boeotian. Aganippe is a fountain in Boeotia, in central Greece, sacred to the Muses.

14 **Maenalus.** See VIII.21n.

15 **Lycaeus.** A mountain in western Arcadia. Said to be the birthplace of Pan and, along with Maenalus, one of his favorite haunts.

18 **Adonis.** A beautiful youth, beloved of Aphrodite (Venus). When he was killed by a boar during a hunt, anemones sprang from his blood. The gods allowed him to spend six months in the underworld and six months upon earth with Aphrodite. Vergil makes him a shepherd for the sake of the pastoral, probably because the Greek pastoral poet Bion had celebrated his death in a famous elegy.

20 **dripping from the winter acorns.** Acorns were steeped in water and used as feed for cattle during the winter months.

21 **Apollo.** See III.103n.

24 **Silvanus.** A Latin god of forests and the country.

26 **Pan.** See II.32n.

26 **Arcadia.** See IV.58n.

36 **Amyntas.** See II.36n.

36 **Phyllis.** See III.75n.

44 **Mars.** See IX.12n.

46 **Alpine.** Of the Alps, a mountain range in central Europe.

47 **Rhine.** The great river of Germany.

49–50 **verse of Chalcis.** The poetry of Euphorion of Chalcis on the island of Euboea, in central Greece, which Gallus had apparently imitated in his earlier days. These may have been *epyllia* (little epics) or love elegies. Setting them for a "Sicilian shepherd's pipe" means writing pastoral instead.

56 **Parthenian.** Of Parthenius, a mountain of Arcadia.

58 **Cydonian.** Cretan. The Cydonians were an ancient people of northwestern Crete. The name was sometimes used of Cretans in general.

58 **Parthian**. See I.63n.

61 **hamadryads**. Wood nymphs.

64 **Hebrus**. A river of Thrace, in northern Greece.

66 **Ethiopian**. Of Ethiopia, the African country south of Egypt.

68 **Pieria**. See III.84n.

75 **Hesperus**. The same as Vesper, the evening and morning star, that is, the planet Venus.